NO
THANKS
I'LL

R. P. JUDSON

WESTBOW
PRESS®
A DIVISION OF THOMAS NELSON
& ZONDERVAN

WestBow Press books may be ordered through booksellers or by contacting:

WestBow Press
A Division of Thomas Nelson & Zondervan
1663 Liberty Drive
Bloomington, IN 47403
www.westbowpress.com
844-714-3454

ISBN: 978-1-6642-7313-9 (sc)
ISBN: 978-1-6642-7314-6 (e)

Library of Congress Control Number: 2022913186

Print information available on the last page.

WestBow Press rev. date: 09/14/2022

To my wife, family, and friends I will ever be grateful.

CONTENTS

ACKNOWLEDGMENTS

I would like to state from the beginning that parts of this book could be interpreted as bragging or prideful. I would like to assure you that they are not. My bragging would be on the Lord who makes all things possible, especially the functionality that I have after a spinal cord injury and many years later breaking my neck in two places. As I have lived and continue to live with the effects of those injuries, I am fully aware of God's goodness and mercy. I can take credit for nothing other than listening to Him and doing my best to follow His lead for my life.

Chapter 1

IT'S A BEAUTIFUL DAY

What an incredible day. We don't get many days like this, I thought. Who would have thought that I would be working in a T-shirt outdoors in Minnesota in the middle of October? It was seventy degrees, and the sun was shining. This was a good thing because I had a lot of work ahead.

I was working for a recreational facility for mentally disadvantaged adults in a whatever-was-needed-at-that-moment type of position. I was the manager, maintenance person, and pastor. The main lodge needed repairs, and I had waited until the season was finished to start some of the major work that needed to be done. One of the projects was to build a new deck on the porch under a lean-to-style roof that covered the deck for an expanse of roughly thirty feet. The lodge sat on a lot with the porch facing an incredible view of the lake. Many of our staff and residents loved sitting on the porch overlooking the lake. This time of year was particularly beautiful, as the fall colors surrounded the lake.

With the help of a crew, we removed the porch deck. They left when that part of the job was done, and I was on my own to rebuild it. That didn't bother me. I really enjoyed the quietness of the camp when it was empty as it was then. It took me about a week to frame the deck, and the Lord had provided unusually good weather for that week. It was Friday morning, and it was a picture-perfect day. I couldn't have ordered a more perfect day. It was one of those days when you just love your job, and you can't wait to get started.

After I had the deck framed, I noticed a pronounced sag near the middle of the overhanging roof. I wanted to replace the posts that kept the roof up, so I was going to level the roof during that process. I looked around at what I had available to do this. I lacked the correct tools for the job, but I never let those things stop me. In the maintenance shed, I had a hydraulic jack that I used to maintain different mowers, tractors, and such on the property. I thought that if I used a two-by-six to reach the rim joist on the roof, I could jack it up and pin it with the new posts I was going to put up.

It seemed like a good plan. After all, what could go wrong? All the original posts were still in place, so the roof couldn't fall on me. I did weigh the risks because I was working alone, but I wanted to raise it only about eight inches, so I thought everything should be fine. I placed the jack directly under the roof, placed the two-by-six between the roof and the jack, and started pumping the jack. It was working perfectly. As I pumped the handle on the jack, the sag in the roof raised. The only issue was that I had to look away from the jack and focus on the roof so that I could see when it would level out. Everything was going according to plan. I was very close to the point that I could put in the new support post, as the roof was nearly level. However, I wasn't able to watch the jack and the roof, and I didn't see that the jack was slipping out from under the two-by-six. The jack slipped out, and the roof came down. As it did, I was able to sort of block it with my arm, but the roof pushed my head down into my neck like an accordion player squeezing an accordion and knocked me to the ground.

I sat on the ground bewildered by what had just happened. I thought, *this is a good time for a coffee break.* There was a nearby picnic table, so I sat at the table, drank some coffee, and once again thought about what a beautiful day it was. I also thought about what had just happened. I thanked the Lord that I wasn't killed. It was a good thing that I'd left the old supports in place, or I would have been flattened like a pancake.

Break time was over; it was time to get back to work. The second time around, I was able to level the roof, and I stood back and thought, *What's next?* I had noticed that the rafters looked rotted as I was jacking the roof up, so I thought I had better inspect them. Sure enough, twelve of them were rotten, but only about a foot on the ends; the rest of them were solid. I decided that it didn't make sense to rebuild the entire roof, and there was no budget to do that, so I would nail two feet of a sister joist on each rafter to repair the rotted section. I cut twelve sister joists, and while I was cutting with the chop saw, I noticed my right shoulder felt funny. There was even had a bit of pain when I moved my arm. I didn't think much about it and started hammering in the sister joists with a twenty-two-ounce framing hammer.

By the time I got done with the last joist, the top of my right shoulder felt like it was on fire and was very painful. I wondered whether I'd torn a rotator cuff or something because my shoulder was really bothering me. Well, it was quitting time, and it was Friday, so I would go home, ice it, and rest it over the weekend. It should be as good as new by Monday—or so I thought. That wasn't the case.

Chapter 2

PAIN

*B*y the time Monday morning came, my shoulder had become very painful, so I thought I had better report the accident to my boss. She was very understanding and told me to get checked out by a doctor. I called to get an appointment. It took a few days to get in, but I managed to keep working by taking my time and using my left hand as much as I could.

When I got to see my doctor, I told him I thought I may have torn my rotator cuff. The doctor put me through a few tests and then told me he didn't think it was a rotator cuff injury but a neck injury. I told him that my neck hurt some, but it was my shoulder that was really painful. He ordered a test to x-ray and scope the inside of my shoulder, which showed normal wear and tear for a forty-three-year-old who had played sports and done a lot of arm wrestling and martial arts over the years. Nothing significant there. Next, he ordered a CT scan, which showed damage to the disks in my neck. This led to me having an MRI.

I had never had an MRI before, and I felt like I had just been closed inside a coffin. I don't know how a person who is claustrophobic can handle one of those. I had to lie motionless for about an hour in this tube with the banging of the machine swirling around my head.

About a week later, I met with a neurosurgeon about the MRI. He said that I had a ruptured disk at C4-C5; a bulging disk at C5-C6; and multilateral tears. I would need surgery: an anterior discectomy at C4-C5. An anterior discectomy, he explained, is where they remove a disk, fill it in with a cadaver bone plug, and cover it with a titanium plate and a couple of screws. He told me that the recovery time would be about three months. I was told that they would go through the front of my neck (the throat area) and pin my voice box over to one side while they performed the discectomy. There would be about a 5 percent chance that I would be hoarse for the rest of my life. As a singer, musician, and pastor, I did not find this very encouraging. I was in a band with my two sons, and we had just started receiving radio play in about forty independent markets around the United States, so that option seemed risky.

I asked the doctor what would happen if I waited on the surgery. He said that the pain would get worse; eventually I would lose feeling and possibly the use of my right arm. Naturally, I asked for a timetable, which he could not give me. He said when I started feeling numbness, I would need to have the surgery right away.

I opted to wait and made many trips to my chiropractor. I entitled this chapter "Pain" because he (pain) became my constant companion. My daily routine was two ibuprofen at breakfast, lunch, supper, and bedtime. It was a very trying time in my life. I was balancing preaching at church, managing the camp, performing with our band STORM, and being a spokesman for a Christian organization raising monthly sponsorships for children in Africa—all with a blown-out neck. Throughout this time, the Lord gave me strength to carry on. In 2005, I was able to travel to Africa and witness our feeding and school programs in Zambia and preach while I was there.

Our Christian band was also very busy, as we had cracked the top ten in several regional radio markets and were playing as main-stage artists at some of the largest festivals in the country.

All the time, I was acutely aware that I was getting close to having to have the surgery.

Chapter 3

BAD NEWS GETS WORSE

$\mathcal{I}$ was able to struggle along for three years from the time I was diagnosed before I had the surgery. That time was extended by my chiropractor, who was a godsend. I saw him at first monthly, then every two weeks and then for the last year I was adjusted weekly. After seeing him so often, we had gotten friendly, and he was very concerned about my injury. He started telling me about six months in advance that he didn't know how much longer I should wait and that he was getting uncomfortable adjusting me. I begged him to keep adjusting me, telling him how he had kept me off the operating table.

Then the day came when the bad news got worse. He adjusted me and as I sat up, he looked at me with a serious look in his eyes and said, "I can't adjust you anymore." I asked him to continue. He said he couldn't. I said I would sign a waiver where he would have no responsibility. He then said, "As a friend, I am telling you it is time to get it fixed and that there is no way I will adjust you again." I knew he meant it and I knew he was right, but I didn't want to admit it. The time had come to see the neurosurgeon again.

Chapter 4
A FLEETING GLIMMER OF HOPE

I called the neurosurgeon and told him what my chiropractor had said. He agreed but offered another option to try, which I was very excited about. He said they would try a steroid injection in my neck around the injured disk. I was not excited about having a needle stuck in my neck, but I figured it couldn't hurt any worse than what I was feeling already, so I was game. On the day of the injection, a friend drove me to the clinic where they would perform the procedure. He asked if I was nervous. I wasn't. I knew the Lord was with me and if He was going to use this injection to help, I was all for it.

I was pleasantly surprised that they numbed the injection site before sticking the rather large needle in my neck. It wasn't that bad—a little pain, but more pressure than pain. When the doctor finished, I asked, "Now what?"

He said, "If it works, it could take up to three days to get any effect from it." I thanked him and started getting dressed. I found my friend in the waiting room and we headed for the car. As we walked to the parking lot, it was like a light switch had just been shut off. The pain in my arm and neck was gone. Three years of almost non-stop pain had abruptly ended. I stopped in the middle of the parking lot and said to my friend, "You're not going to believe this. I am pain free; it worked." It had only been about twenty minutes and I was without pain and thanking God. I can't express how I felt after having such pain for so long and suddenly having none. I was ecstatic.

The chapter is called "A Fleeting Glimmer of Hope." I say fleeting because as quickly as the injection gave relief, it failed. Three days later, while I was at work painting one of the cabins at the property, the pain returned like a sledgehammer. What I thought was a cure turned out to be short-lived. I was devastated and angry, knowing that this meant surgery. I was about to get an education in dealing with workers' compensation, hospitals, and lawyers that I will never forget. The following events took years to sort through, and I am living with residual effects to this day.

Chapter 5

YOU'RE JUST A NUMBER

*H*ave you ever felt like you are a number caught up in the big machine? It's all about profit and loss: the least amount of cost for the most minimal amount of care allowed by law. A short time after the injection, I was contacted by an irate workers' comp representative. The representative wanted to know how I had received an injection in my neck without his blessing. I had no idea that my doctor had not received or even asked permission for the steroid injection in my neck. I didn't even know that it was required.

The workers' comp representative said that they would not pay for the injection unless I agreed to see a different neurologist. I didn't really care who I saw and assumed that all neurologists must be qualified. The workers' comp representative also asked me if I would be willing to try more rehabilitation instead of surgery. I liked that idea, so he sent me to one of their preferred doctors. This rehab doctor was very personable, and he and I hit it off right from the beginning. We discussed my injury but also many aspects of life. I was a pastor, and he was Jewish, and we had great conversations.

That relationship did not last long. I met him for rehab twice a week, but after three months and an electromyography (EMG) test, he said there was nothing he could do for me. He said that I had exhausted everything I could try and that the time had come to have the surgery. I didn't want to hear that, but I knew that he was right. The pain and the numbness in my fingers meant the time had come. My rehab doctor told me that he had a surgeon in mind who was recommended by workers' comp. I said I would go with whomever they recommended. That turned out to be a big mistake. Remember that the title of this chapter is "You're Just a Number"? I was about to learn all about that and start a journey that continues as I write this book. I can now say, with hindsight as a guide, that you should always get a second opinion and never just trust those who carry the title of expert. Keep in mind that an expert is just someone who has checked all the boxes indicating that he or she is an expert. Those boxes are questions developed by mere humans who are very capable of committing errors.

Chapter 6

THE "GENIUS"

*B*efore I met with this surgeon, my neurologist and workers' comp rep warned me that the neurosurgeon I was about to meet was abrupt, a little disheveled at times, and arrogant, but that he was the one I wanted. He was a "genius"—their word, not mine. My wife and I met with him, and the descriptions were accurate. He was abrupt, he was disheveled, and I remember thinking his hair was like Albert Einstein's if he hadn't combed it and had dyed it black. He was arrogant—boy, was he arrogant. He told me he would be performing an interior discectomy at level C4-C5; he would be removing the disk, filling the space with a bone plug made from cadaver bone, and securing it all with a titanium plate and two screws. He said that it was simple for him; he had done hundreds of these operations, and he was the best there was. His arrogance was reassuring in a strange way; he seemed extremely confidant. He told me I would go in on Monday and be home on Tuesday. I would have about three months of rehab and I would be like new.

This prognosis was exactly what I wanted to hear. I had a large renovation project at the camp starting three months after the scheduled surgery. I needed to oversee that project and bow hunting season was starting two weeks after that. My fall season was completely booked and there was no time for any delays. This, I would discover later, was one of the things God was trying to tell me: I was way too busy and guilty of overbooking myself often. Nevertheless, I would always find a way to get things done. I had no problem putting thirty-six hours of work into a twenty-four-hour day. I would be working on several things at one time and then say, "Look at all that I am doing for the Lord." I didn't realize I was doing several things with mediocrity instead of listening to the Lord and doing a couple of things with His excellence. At the time of my injury, I was managing the handicapped care camp, working as the national child sponsorship director for children in Africa, playing in an up-and-coming Christian band that was getting radio play, and pastoring a church. I will talk more about all that later. To say I was busy would be an understatement. I thought I was honoring the Lord by doing all this.

Back to the "genius" neurosurgeon. Although he had all the attributes I had been warned about, I thought that if this surgery had to be done, I wanted it to be done quickly so I could get on with my life. He sounded so absolute on my quick recovery that he sold me. I was scheduled for the surgery. The surgery date was to be June 6, 2006; in other words, it would be 6/6/06. A week before the surgery, I had to have a physical. Since I knew I was going to be out of commission for a couple of months, I wanted to have some fun. The guys and I went out paintballing. If you don't know what playing paintball is, let me quickly explain. You fire round balls filled with paint from a gun powered by CO_2 gas cartridges. When you are hit, the paint splatters, marking you out of that round. Being the testosterone-driven males that we were, of course we cranked up the power, so we felt it when we were hit.

Thank God some wisdom has come with my years and outlived my machoism. When I showed up for the physical, the doctor asked what I had done to get all the massive bruises. When I told him about paintball, he said if that was fun, then leave him out. Once again, in hindsight, I would have to agree. The night before the surgery, my whole family took me to Pirate's Cove to play mini golf, one of my favorite past times. Little did I know it would be the last time I would be able to enjoy a time like this with my family for a long time. It was the calm before the storm.

Chapter 7

THE DAY THAT LIFE CHANGED FOREVER

The morning of the surgery was frenzied. My wife was supposed to be able to come to see me in pre-op and she was never given the opportunity. The people who had been scheduled for surgery were lined up like on an assembly line; everything was rushed. When my wife asked when she could see me, the staff told her that things had been moved up and I was heading into surgery. I remember that prior to the surgery I had electrodes attached to my head, neck, arms, and legs. I was told they would be monitoring my spinal cord pressure throughout the procedure. For those who have never had surgery, it is much like you see on TV. I was given a shot to relax me. A few minutes later, they put a mask over my nose and mouth and told me to count backwards from ten. I think I made it to eight and I was out.

I awoke to a nurse telling me to wake up. It was hard to wake up. I was very groggy. As I became aware of where I was, I tried to move my legs, but I couldn't. Then I tried to lift my arms and I couldn't do that either. At first, I thought I must not be awake. It seemed very strange, surreal. It felt like I was in between dreaming and being awake. As the nurse continued to wake me, I told her that

I couldn't move or feel my legs or arms. I saw panic on her face. She said it was the aftereffects of the anesthesia but that she would get the doctor. The surgeon came in and was very rude, acting like I had done something wrong and told me that it would wear off. Thirty minutes later, it hadn't "worn off," so I was rushed in for a CT scan. The CT scan, we found out later, was not the test I needed. I should have had an MRI, but the "genius" had his reason for avoiding that. The CT scan showed what he wanted to see, that the bone plug was not pressing against my spinal cord. He then said that my spinal cord had swollen, that the swelling would go down very soon, and I would be back to normal. It was one of many lies that I would be told over the course of the next three months.

That night was a long night for my family and myself. We were all in disbelief. This surgery that was supposed to be routine for this surgeon turned out to be not so routine. Suddenly I was able to move very slowly, like a turtle walking through molasses. I could not feel anything, but I was gaining movement. I still had no feeling from my neck down to my toes, but I was at least moving slightly. I was heavily sedated and fell into a drug-induced sleep until morning.

When I woke the next day, I felt like I had a nightmare that lasted all night, but it wasn't a nightmare—it was all too real. My faith in the Lord and my trust in the surgeon gave me hope. I remembered that the surgeon told me that my spinal cord was just swollen, and I would regain everything once the swelling went down. I had no reason not to believe him at that point. I trusted in his expertise and besides, bad things didn't happen to good people—or at least that's what I hoped for. I was sure that I would be fine at any moment.

Day 1

Day one was so strange. I was trying to play guitar chords in the air to see if I thought I could ever play guitar again. My daughter said it looked like I was a marionette with someone else working the strings because my movements were so slow and uncontrolled. It was also time to try walking. Walking without being able to feel my legs or my feet and literally having to tell each leg to move was difficult and unnatural. People would ask how I was doing that or how it felt. The best description I could come up with was that it was like having large water balloons strapped to your feet and trying to balance and walk. One trip to the bathroom and I would be exhausted. It took so much effort. I felt very weak. I had no idea how weak I really was. I spent most of my time in a wheelchair that first day but was told that I would be starting physical therapy on day two. I was excited about that. I was all for anything that would speed up the recovery.

Day 2

Therapy day. I started out with a small hallway walk; a therapist wrapped a belt around my waist and held me as I walked. I felt bad because I was around two hundred and eighty pounds and most of my therapists were not even half my weight. I was never concerned about my weight. I knew I was heavy, but I was also active. I coached basketball and taught a self-defense class in two different high schools. I held a third-degree black belt in Kenpo and had been an athlete all my life. I was really into lifting weights. The week before the surgery, I was in the weight room at the high school teasing the kids on the football team because I could outlift them. At age forty-three, I could still bench three hundred pounds. That's one of the reasons I was never concerned about my weight. I always thought that if there was ever a time in my life that I couldn't at least bench my own body weight, then I would lose weight.

Reality was about to come crashing down in my first therapy session. I was in my wheelchair, and I was in a class where everybody else was seventy or older. Our therapist handed each one of us three-pound weights. All we were supposed to do was turn them over and back in our hands. I couldn't do it with my right hand; with my left hand, I flipped the weight over, but I didn't have the hand strength to hold it I dropped the weight in my lap. I was devastated. How could this be? How was this possible? How could I go from being strong and healthy to being the weakest person in a class of senior saints?

I was allowed to rest for a couple of hours before my next walking therapy session. This time I went into a room where I was holding onto parallel bars with a mirror on the end, just like you see in the movies. All that I could think about as I watched myself trying to walk using the parallel bars is that I saw this in a movie. This could not be happening to me—none of this could be happening to me. I had to keep telling myself that this was only temporary. Soon the swelling in my spinal cord would go down and everything would go back to normal.

Day 3

I learned many things from this injury. On the third day, something I had never doubted or lacked in took hold of me. I lost my confidence. I was a very confident person prior to this. The year before the surgery, I grabbed a couple of suitcases and flew halfway around the world to preach and teach in Africa. I traveled around London by myself with no concerns, handing out tracts and sharing the gospel.

When I was twenty-five, I was promoted at work as the forestry products divisional manager at the world's largest sporting goods manufacturer. We made baseball bats for retailers like Walmart, Toys R Us, Dick's Sporting Goods, Major League Baseball, and many others. I had no idea what I was doing, but I had confidence in the Lord and so I succeeded. After ten years, I took my family and moved halfway across the United States. I was the plant manager for a high-tech manufacturing company with one hundred and forty employees working under me. Again, it was a situation where my confidence in the Lord gave me the abilities I needed to succeed.

The Lord has always blessed me with good jobs, so I would

pastor small churches that couldn't afford a pastor. My corporate life enabled me to help those churches. Now that confidence was gone. I was humbled, broken both physically and mentally. I was dependent on others for many things in my life that I took for granted. I wasn't even able to dress myself. I was never one to ask anyone for help. I always did it myself; that way I knew it would be done right. I learned how the Lord could change that in a person. Simple things, like brushing my teeth, were struggles. To this day, I need use a large handled toothbrush and I must hold it awkwardly just to brush my teeth.

I have provided counseling for many years, and I could never understand why people who were so confident could have something like a heart attack or cancer and lose all their confidence and bravado. I understood it at that point. Mine was gone. I was fearful—fearful of what I would do for the rest of my life. I felt like I had nothing to offer any longer. I lay awake that night after my family had gone and prayed for the Lord to heal me and give me direction. When I pray, I always find peace with God, knowing He is listening. This time I felt no peace, no direction, and very little hope. Then I remembered that all this was just temporary. The swelling in my spinal cord would go down and I would go back to work, back to my church, and back to my normal life. This would be the pattern for me for the next three months. I would get caught up in the despair and then tell myself that it was just temporary.

Day 4

Day four was a rinse and repeat of the previous day: get up, eat breakfast, and have my first physical therapy session of the day. My doctor and the "genius" surgeon would come in and spend five minutes with me, telling me that at any time I would start returning to normal and regain full function of my arms and legs. I didn't know it at the time, but at least one of those two was either a very good liar or delusional. Many years later, as I write this book, I know the answer to that question. The "genius" was a very good liar *and* very delusional. Two things can be true at the same time.

There was something else happening that I didn't really notice until about the fourth day. I was asked by a shift nurse every day throughout the day if I felt angry, like I might lose control. I finally asked why everyone kept asking me that same question. After everything I had been through, some of the medication I was on could make me cranky. I would find out about a month after I was released what they were talking about. I will discuss in an upcoming chapter what happened when I exploded in anger at my family. The nurses had good reason to ask me because they knew what they were pumping into my system to try to control the "swelling" in my spinal cord. This was another lie. There was never any swelling in my spinal cord. I will also cover that in a later chapter.

Day 5

This is the hardest part of this book for me to write. There is no way to properly articulate what happened the night of day five in the hospital, but here is my attempt. The day started like all the other days: breakfast, therapy, and a visit from the "genius" and the doctor telling me that at any time I would be back to normal. (That story was getting old, but I believed them because they were the experts, or so I thought.) Then there was afternoon therapy and visits with family. Thank God for them and my two dear brothers in the Lord who brought me encouragement every day. My days were blending together.

I remember lying in my bed praying for the nightmare to be over. I prayed that I would wake up and be healed. I kept my fear hidden. After all, I had to be strong for my family and friends. I kept telling them that I was fine, and everything would be all right, while inside I had a feeling of dread, as if I knew something was wrong. I thought, *what if I don't heal anymore? What can I possibly do for the rest of my life?* I drifted off to sleep with all these thoughts swirling in my head.

I don't know exactly what time this happened, and I can't explain what happened. I very much felt like what the apostle Paul wrote about in 2 Corinthians 12:2–4

> I know a man in Christ who fourteen years ago was caught up to the third heaven. Whether it was in the body or out of it I do not know, but God knows. And I know that this man—whether in the body or out of it I do not know, but God knows—was caught up to Paradise. The things he heard were too sacred for words, things that man is not permitted to tell.

Like Paul, I do not know, but I can say that I was in the presence of God. The Lord was standing by my side; there was no pain, but instead absolute joy and peace and a light so intense but not painful to look at. I was standing in awe basking in this euphoria when a voice said to me, "Do you need your arms and legs to love Me?"

I answered, "No Lord." I was overcome and weeping.

I was asked a second time, "Do you need your arms and legs to love Me?"

I answered again, "No Lord."

A third time I was asked, "Do you need your arms and legs to love me?"

I answered a third time, "No Lord." The rest of this encounter with the Lord is also as Paul's. There are things not to be shared.

I woke to a nurse asking me if I was all right. I could see fear in her eyes, and I realized that I was still weeping, soaked with tears, to the point where I had to change my hospital gown. I regained my composure enough to assure her I was okay. She took my vitals and was amazed that my blood pressure, oxygen levels, and temperature were perfect considering how I looked. My tears were of unbelievable love, not remorse or fear, and that's why my vitals were perfect.

People who know me and read this book will be surprised by my encounter with the Lord because I have never experienced supernatural events and am very skeptical when I hear such stories. No one could be more conservative in his or her spiritual or overall life in general than I am.

Everything changed from that point. I knew that God was with me in this, and I was being trained by this injury. Hebrews 12:11 states, "Now no chastening seems to be joyful for the present, but painful; nevertheless, afterward it yields the peaceable fruit of righteousness to those who have been trained by it."

I was going to be trained by this injury rather than have it overcome me. I have had to remind myself of that many, many times over the years, as there are days of pain and loss of ability that hinder me still and that will increase as I grow older. The truth today is the same as the truth when my injury happened and will be the same truth in the years to come. That truth—that the love of the Lord will sustain me—carries me through. I also know that if the time comes when I no longer have the use of my arms or legs, I do not need them to love God, and I know regardless of my state that He loves me.

I have only shared this experience with a handful of people. I am a little apprehensive about sharing it in this book, but it seems this is the time the Lord had chosen for me to share what has happened. This experience has been what has sustained me through the many years since the surgery.

Day 6

I was still in a rinse and repeat cycle: same procedures, same questions, same answers, same visitors, same fake smiles, same lies. My hope and strength now rested in my experience from the day before. Before I went to sleep that night, I prayed the Lord would visit me again like the previous night. I have prayed that prayer again many times since, wanting just a taste of that peace and love once again, but it hasn't happened. I know this: there is no earthly joy that compares to what God shared with me that night.

It was at this point that I started asking why I couldn't be discharged. I was no longer on an IV. I was taking meds in pill form and doing physical therapy once a day. The other twenty-three hours, I was lying in a hospital bed. I explained that my wife could give me my meds and drive me to physical therapy. It was one mile from my home. I was told that I needed to be observed in the hospital for a few more days. I reluctantly agreed.

Days 7 and 8

Same old, same old.

Day 9

This day started like every other day—same questions, same lies, same false pleasantries exchanged—although I had been asking for three days why I couldn't be discharged.

This day did have a twist. I was alerted that one of my parishioners had been brought in during the night after a motorcycle accident. Fortunately, he was not seriously injured. The nurse did allow me to go to his room in my wheelchair and visit with him. I finally felt like I was doing something. It was very uplifting to share some hope with someone else. His injuries were minor, so he was released after one day.

Day 10

I was very frustrated at this point. I was sitting in my room twenty-three hours a day, doing the same routine with the same results, and seeing no improvement. My daily conversations with the "genius" and my doctor were the same as they had been ten days before. They kept saying my spinal cord was swollen, it would go down, and I would be back to normal.

Day 11

In the words of REO Speed Wagon, it was time for me to fly. In came the medical team with the same questions, same lies, same everything. My response was the only thing that changed. I again told them that I was capable of leaving the hospital, that my wife could administer my meds, and that she could take me to therapy. Once again, they said no and that I needed more observation. Wrong answer. I said that they had been calling me by my first name while I referred to them as doctors, but that was no longer on the table. They would need to refer to me as Pastor Judson. I explained that Pastor Judson would be signing himself out of the hospital that day, there would be no further discussion, and they should prepare the release papers.

The "genius" and my doctor looked a little stunned but finally agreed that we could do everything from my home that they were doing for me in the hospital.

My release time was set for two o'clock that afternoon. A couple came to my room to visit, and a God thing happened while they were there. When I went into the hospital, I didn't take my Bible. At the time, I thought I was only going to be there overnight and there was always one in the room anyway. I didn't know that I would end up being there eleven days. I found out that I didn't need my Bible as my daughter wrote out scripture verse posters for my wall and my two brothers from different mothers, Bill and Jon, came daily to my room and shared scripture with me. They are both awesome, Godly men and were a huge encouragement to me.

Back to the God thing. As I was visiting with this couple, a black bird came to my windowsill and started pecking at the window. My friend commented, "I have never seen a crow in this area. How strange." It was a stark contrast as we usually only saw sea gulls. I immediately thought of the story in 1 Kings chapter 17 where the Lord used ravens to feed Elijah. I hadn't brought my Bible, but the Lord sent people to feed me His word. I saw it as conformation that God would always take care of me.

Chapter 8

A FREE MAN

$\mathcal{I}$ was going home. It was an intensely sunny day when I left the hospital. I felt the sun and the wind for the first time in eleven days. It was awesome. When I got home, it didn't take long to realize that although it was great to be out of my hospital room things were incredibly difficult. Many things that we all take for granted I could no longer do by myself. One of the first humbling experiences I had was trying to dress in everyday clothes. In the hospital, I wore a hospital gown. That was easy to get on and off. Clothing and shoes were another thing. The man who had traveled halfway around the world to preach and teach the gospel would now have to ask for help to put on a pair of shoes.

I could no longer drive an automobile. At this point, I would like to tell you a little about the angel that I married. I was only sixteen years-old and she was eighteen when we married. My mother was the only one who thought it would last so she gave me permission to get married. Everyone said it wouldn't last a year. She was a good girl, and I was a trouble-making brawler who loved to drink, fight, and play in heavy metal bands. She saw something in me no one else saw and she stuck with me. We were both saved seven years after we were married and that changed my life for the better. We just celebrated our forty-second wedding anniversary. I guess my mom was right and everyone else was wrong. My wife is unbelievable. She nursed me back to health and continues to be my nurse years later, as my spinal cord injury has involved other areas of my body and required major surgeries. If there is anyone in this story who deserves an award or accolades besides God, it would be her.

I was required to go to therapy three times a week and see my general practitioner every week. He, unlike the "genius," was a good and kind man. He genuinely cared about my wellbeing.

I had been home about two weeks when I realized why I kept being asked while in the hospital if I felt angry or like I might lose control. Both of those things happened to me. I was taking a shower and because of my lack of hand control, I dropped the shampoo bottle and it made a loud noise. My wife started pounding on the bathroom door asking me if I was all right.

I completely blew up. I let her help me get dressed and then I went out into the living room and yelled at my family, telling them to stop treating me like a five-year old. It was completely out of character. I had a rage I had never felt before. After the incident was over and I calmed down, I remembered that I had been asked over and over if I felt like I was going to lose control. Well, I did, and I didn't like it. I decided to start doing some research on what drugs I had been taking as I felt out of sorts most of the time. One of the drugs I discovered was a very potent steroid, one that comes with a warning of sudden outbursts of anger. It was not recommended that anyone take the drug more than ten days. I had been on it twenty. This was given to take the supposed swelling out of my spinal cord. It never did because that was not the problem.

On top of the steroid, I was taking Gabapentin, Percocet, an antibiotic, and hydrocodone. Not only was I suffering from the spinal cord injury, I was also very sick and having an allergic reaction to the Percocet. It took three weeks before this was figured out. I remember going to sleep wondering if I would wake up. There were several mornings I was surprised that I woke up and I was more than fine if the Lord took me home in my sleep. I would say to myself, *I can't believe I am still here.*

Chapter 9
THE PLOT THICKENS

$\mathcal{I}$ had been out of the hospital a month and having therapy and weekly visits with my regular doctor, who was one of the good guys. He said he wished he had a magic wand he could wave and heal me because he could see how miserable and sick I was. I was covered in a rash from the allergy to Percocet on top of all the issues from my spinal cord. My doctor told me that I should have gotten better by that point. He ordered an MRI; this was something that should have been done right after the surgery when I was experiencing post-operative complications.

I also had to have a follow up visit with the "genius," my surgeon. When I went to his office, I was barely able to walk with the aid of a walker and I used a wheelchair much of the time. The "genius" looked at an x-ray, said that I was doing well, and that I could go back to work with a fifty-pound lifting restriction. My wife and I were in disbelief. I explained that I couldn't even lift a gallon jug of milk or walk more than a few feet. He became extremely rude, said he had people he needed to see, and ushered us out. We were in shock as to how we were treated.

At my next physical therapy session, I mentioned the incident to my physical therapists, two angels of mercy, who were excellent and helped me so much in my recovery. They said they were not surprised. They told me that he had a reputation for being extremely rude and arrogant. They also said that he makes more "mistakes" than any surgeon they had ever seen, and people were being permanently injured from what should be routine surgeries. They laughed out loud when I told them that he had been referred to me as a genius. They said they had filed several complaints to their superiors asking for an investigation to be done on him, but nothing ever happened.

Back to the MRI. Because my doctor was in the same health care system as my surgeon, he saw that my doctor had ordered an MRI, so he ordered a test of his own, an EMG. There was a lot going on at this time. I had a lawyer who was helping me set up my worker's compensation claim. The lawyer said that he had been in the business over thirty years, and he had never seen a case like mine. He said I needed to get a second opinion outside of the healthcare system I was in because I should have been much better by that point. I told him I would think about it, but I still trusted the surgeon. I still believed that my spinal cord was just swollen, and I would return to normal.

It was on a Friday when I was to have the MRI and the EMG. The MRI was what they call a wet and dry MRI. I would have a standard MRI and then one with contrasting dye. That was in the morning and the EMG was in the afternoon. An EMG is where they stick you with pins from one part of your body to another, send an electric signal between the two pins, and measure the return signal time. It is not a very pleasant test.

As the test was being administered, the doctor received a call which he took while he worked on me. He said to the person on the other end of the line, "Yes, I am working on him right now. That is consistent with what I am finding." He said a few more things and then hung up.

I told him I assumed the conversation was about me, and he said it was. I asked what it was that he found consistent with the earlier

MRI. He told me he couldn't discuss that with me, and I would have to speak to the surgeon.

When I left the hospital that afternoon, I was confused and a little worried about what they had found but not shared with me. I did a lot of praying that night.

On Saturday morning, I received a phone call from a number that I didn't recognize but I did recognize the voice on the other end of the line. It was my regular doctor, one of the good guys. He told me he was calling me from his home, but he had to speak to me regarding the MRI results and that he couldn't sleep another night without talking to me. He said that he found something on the MRI, that it was serious, and he wanted me to be examined outside of my current healthcare system because he feared there was a cover-up going on and I needed help immediately. I guessed my lawyer's suspicions were correct.

I spoke to a friend who got me an appointment with a neurotrauma surgeon in one of the best hospitals in the state. He was the head of neurology for this hospital and highly regarded in his profession. He was booked for a month, so I took the first appointment I could get with him. It was a two-and-a-half-hour drive to his office.

Chapter 10
THE TRUTH HURTS

$\mathcal{I}$ was now three months beyond the initial surgery with no improvement, little to no feeling in both legs and both arms, and there was little to no feeling in my pinky, ring, and middle fingers on both hands. I was having difficulty walking with a walker and was spending most of my time in a wheelchair. I also had extreme spasms in my right ribcage where the muscles would all tense up, making it hard to breathe. This is very painful.

If it were not for the Lord in my life, I do not know how I would have gotten through those first three months and every day since then.

It was the day to meet this new specialist. He had already seen all the data from the MRI and the EMG. He brought the image of the MRI up on the screen for my wife and me to see. There was a side-by-side image of pre-surgery MRI and post-surgery MRI. I don't have a medical degree but there was an obvious problem between the pre- and post-MRI images. To me, the post-MRI looked like a there was a white eraser smudge across my spinal cord.

The specialist said that the "smudge" was where the surgeon, a.k.a. "the genius," had cut my spinal cord during the surgery. He said that it was a miracle that I could move at all, that I should be a complete quadriplegic paralyzed from the ears down. He explained that it was no different than being in an auto accident, that my spinal cord was damaged at C4-C5, and that there was no way I should be able to move. I have seen many doctors who have said the exact same thing: it was a miracle, and I should be paralyzed. I guess the Lord had a different plan.

The doctor was then very blunt. He reiterated that this was no different than if I had been in an auto accident, that it was a spinal cord injury, and there was no cure. He said to be thankful for what I had, and I would have to learn to live life the way I was because my disability was permanent. My wife broke down crying. I was angry, numb, and trying to comprehend what I just heard. It is amazing how fast the human mind can think. *What now? Is ministry over? Will I ever walk normally again? Will I work? How can I function? Is the band that was getting national radio play now over?* I played the past, present, and future ten years in my head in a matter of seconds. I thanked the doctor for being truthful with us. It was the first time in three months that we hadn't been lied to and given drugs to try and hide the truth. There was something that my wife and I realized and that is that the truth hurts.

It was a very long two-and-a-half-hour car ride home as the prognosis had time to settle in. Life would certainly be different.

Chapter 11

WHY LORD?

$\mathcal{F}$or the first few months after the news, I poured myself into rehab. I was told I had an eighteen-month window where I might gain some motor control and strength. I gave it my all to get as much back as I could. My insurance refused to pay for rehab after nine months so I was rehabbing at home as much as I could. My lawyer had requested more rehab after a six-month hiatus; the insurance company agreed, and I eagerly accepted.

While I worked on my body, I struggled in my mind. Why would God take me out of the game and put me on the bench? I was busy with three full-time ministries, coaching, refereeing basketball, and teaching two self-defense classes. I could not understand why this would happen to me. It was strange because I had no anger toward the "genius" who botched my surgery. I had more anger toward God for allowing it to happen. This feeling would stew within me for years and my anger grew. I never left my beliefs, I never stopped trusting God, but I was angry. I never let anyone know my feelings; after all I was a pastor and a super Christian—how could I dare be angry with God? I got very good at telling people, "I'm okay," with a smile on my face when I was far from okay inside.

I asked the question, "Why Lord?" many times, particularly

in the shower, which was a safe place to pray and a safer place to cry. You can't see tears in the shower. I knew that in 2 Corinthians chapter 12, Paul prayed three times for the thorn in his flesh to be removed. The answer he received was that God's grace was sufficient and that in his weakness, he would be strong. I prayed many times for God to remove my thorn. Paul's answer became my answer, and yet I struggled for meaning in all that was going on. It would be four years before I got my answer from God. I was on His time schedule, not mine.

During this time, I received some of the best advice that I have ever received. By this point, I had switched to a different healthcare system, and I had a very kind elderly man as my neuro rehab specialist. He was old school: no computers. He would take out a yellow legal pad and fill up six sheets of notes at each visit. On one visit, he told me that I had every right to use my wheelchair and electric scooter and that most people in my situation did just that. He cautioned that if I did, my muscles would atrophy and in one month I would not be able to get out of the wheelchair; my immobility would be permanent. My reply was the title of this book: "No thanks, I'll walk." I was determined to heed his advice.

I noticed something my first time out in public in my wheelchair: the view is much different from a wheelchair. This was another motivational factor for trying to leave the wheelchair behind. I used to be the one who would help the little old ladies who couldn't reach an item on the top shelf, now I would only be able to watch helplessly. This was difficult for me to adjust to.

Chapter 12

I GET BY WITH A LITTLE HELP FROM MY FRIENDS

I was dealing with the reality that my independence had been taken away from me. I no longer did things when I wanted to. I got dressed when my wife dressed me. I never had to wait for her, because she was by my side every moment that I needed her. It was difficult for me to accept that I couldn't put on a pair of shoes, button my own shirt, and lots of everyday things that we all take for granted.

One of the big freedoms that I lost was driving a car. I was the guy who grabbed a backpack and traveled halfway around the world preaching and teaching by myself. Now I wasn't even able to walk to the mailbox without someone being with me.

I had to ask people for help to do most things. I had never had to do that before. I had to depend on others. I had to rely on my family and friends for help. I hated this new twist in my life. The Bible tells us that which we see as evil God means it for good. I was being refined, tried, molded, and couldn't see the forest for the trees. Sometimes we are so wrapped up in a moment that we lose sight of what's really going on.

It had been three years since the accident, and I asked my doctor if I could start driving again. He said I should be tested by the state to see if I was capable. The test was simple enough. There was a box with a green light bulb and a red light bulb. It had a gas and a brake pedal. The green light was to accelerate and of course the red light was to brake. A machine measured my reaction time. The lady who administered the test said that I failed to react in the appropriate amount of time, so I failed the reaction test. I was told that there was also an actual driving test; if I passed it, I would be able to keep my license. The car I was to drive had a brake for the person administering the test "just in case." I passed the physical driving test, so it was up to the Department of Transportation whether to take my license or not. I failed one test but passed the other. If I failed, I would have to learn to drive with hand controls and take another driving test. The man who gave me the driving test decided to let me keep my license and suggested that I practice in a parking lot. I was thankful for that.

It would be five years before I was able to drive a car and I am still limited. My wife still does about ninety percent of all our driving.

During this time of my life, I was getting used to allowing people to help me and being okay with it. I started appreciating the fact that people were more than willing to help. The Lord was using a chisel to sculpt what He wanted rather than what I thought He wanted.

Chapter 13
A DARK PLACE

This chapter will be a tough one for me to relive, as it was the lowest point in my life. I have never been good at sharing my emotions. The only time I would share any emotions is when I would get angry enough to blow up. The rest of the time, I pretended that everything was all right. Whenever anyone would ask me how I was doing, I would say all right or that I was fine. I thought that was the response I had to give. I had to be strong for my family and friends. I could not let them see I had doubts about my future.

My biggest struggles were trying to understand why God would abruptly end three strong ministries and what my identity was now. I could not fathom why God would end my ministries. There were people coming to the Lord within the three ministries I was involved in. All seemed well.

For the larger part of my ministry life, I pastored churches that could not afford a full-time pastor. My main income was running businesses up to the corporate level while pastoring. Like Paul's tent making, God has always blessed me with good jobs. My background is in managing manufacturing plants that produce products that went to large companies like Major League Baseball, Walmart, Amazon, and World Bank, just to name a few. As I mentioned earlier, the last company I ran was a high-tech manufacturing facility with over a hundred and forty employees working under me. I share this because of the identity issue I was struggling with. Prior to this accident, I had always been called by my titles. I was always pastor at church, and boss, boss man, or Mr. Judson in business. Now I was nobody. I had had three years of being nobody, not able to work or do much of anything. I never thought about how important my identity was to me. If there was a problem to be solved, people would come to me to solve it; now I had become the problem. In my mind, I had become a burden to my wife and family, yet I was able to put up a front to everyone making them believe I was all right.

On top of everything else, the disability insurance only recognized one of my jobs. My wife and I went from a nearly six-figure income to about two hundred dollars a week. It took two years to get this straightened out. By that time, we lost everything financially.

I had decided that everyone would be better off without me. I had convinced myself that God had taken away my identity and that I was useless to those around me, so what was I living for? I made my plan. I didn't want my wife to have to find my body and I didn't want to make a mess. I decided that I would take the car without my wife knowing, check into a hotel room, write my goodbye letter, take all my pain meds, and drift off and die. No mess, no fuss. I and the world would be better off.

These suicidal fantasies were being worked out in my head for the better part of the third year of my spinal injury. One day while we were driving, I told my wife what I had been thinking. She had a strong suspicion all along that I was struggling. We had a very sobering discussion at that point. Our marriage was strong, and this only made it stronger. It was shortly after confessing my thoughts that the Lord showed me why I was going through all that was happening.

Chapter 14

FORGIVE ME LORD

I was reading in the book of Genesis chapter 50 where Joseph is dealing with his brothers after they had sold him into slavery as a child. Verse twenty really spoke to me: "But as for you, you meant it for evil against me, but God meant it for good." It had been four years since the surgery that changed my life and I thought, *Is it possible that anything good could come out of this? Is there a chance that this situation I was plunged into could possibly be used for good?* I started to pray for the Lord to reveal what I needed to do, or if He was done with me completely. Suddenly, I had clarity of mind.

When I had my dream, vision, visitation with the Lord, or whatever it was, I was asked, "Do you need your arms and legs to love Me"? That thought came back and has come back many times since then. I told the Lord, "No, I do not need my arms and legs to love You." It was then that I truly realized I did not need my arms or legs or anything or anyone else to love God. What happened to me was a blessing in disguise. I thought what was done to me was evil, but it was actually for my good. I was so focused on running under my own power that I never relied on the Lord or anyone else. The Lord knew exactly what needed to be done to get me to stop and wait on Him. I had to be physically forced to stop running twenty-four hours a day and focus on Him.

My ministry had become very works orientated. I looked at what I was doing for the Lord, all those ministries bearing the fruit of salvation. The truth was that each ministry got a portion of my attention and never what God had wanted. I was so lost in the forest of ministry that I couldn't see through the trees. I was too busy patting myself on the back to hear that God wanted me focused on Him rather than the ministries. My ministry life was completely out of balance. I had put the cart before the horse. I was trusting in my work for the Lord instead of trusting in the Lord for my work, if that makes any sense.

I have learned that we can have great intentions in our ministries to serve God and at the same time not spend our own personal time with God. I think we fall into a rut where we mistake ministry time as satisfying our own time fellowshipping with God. We pour and pour into our ministries and forget that we need to go back to the source to be refilled so that we can continue to pour out refreshing drink that satisfies. This can become like a hamster running on his exercise wheel. We run to exhaustion and never really go anywhere.

This is not to diminish in any way what the Lord had done during my ministry. Many people were saved, encouraged, and challenged. The Lord certainly used me during that time despite the blinders I was wearing. I missed the blessing by not taking time to appreciate what God was doing and focusing on what His priority was. I was unwittingly focused on my priority. All I can say is I am thankful we serve a forgiving God and that He can use us despite our many shortcomings.

Chapter 15

RESIDUAL THORNS

The spinal cord injury has had lifelong residual thorns that will be a part of my life forever. I have only about ten percent feeling in both legs, feet, and both arms. I cannot stop hyperextending my knees when I walk. This has caused both knees to wear out. I had my right knee replaced thirteen years after the spinal cord injury and my left knee replaced after the fourteenth year. Both surgeries were challenges. Rehabbing a complete knee replacement is difficult enough, but a spinal cord injury on top of that adds additional challenges. The quadriceps in my thighs have never been the same. The nerves are already damaged from the original injury and now the knee replacement has made them worse. The prosthetic knees that were installed have pins in them that do not allow me to hyperextend them, so that is good. Nevertheless, with all that said, I am able to walk, which is a miracle in itself.

While I was having the MRIs for my knees, I was told that both my hips have also been worn out because of the way I walk so they will also have to be replaced at a future date. The Lord will get me through that also, just as He has been with me every step of the way in my life.

These are the known residual thorns I have. I am sure there will be more as I age. The one thing I know is that as challenges arise, I learn more about myself and more about the Savior and His grace. It seems that with every thorn that appears, the wonderful scent of the rose becomes stronger.

Chapter 16
FRESH CUT GRASS AND DÉJÀ VU

I finished writing this book but waited on publishing it for unknown reasons at that time. I now know why I didn't publish it. It wasn't finished, even though I thought it was.

It was a sunny Saturday morning; my brother was visiting, and I was showing him a four-wheeler I had bought. I planned on using it for plowing my driveway during the coming winter. He took it for a short ride and returned. I was going to put it back in the garage but thought I would take a quick ride and then put it away. I putted down the driveway about a hundred and fifty yards and then punched the gas to get down to the trail back to the garage. When I punched the gas, the machine abruptly turned left. I was completely out of control, up on two wheels, and heading straight into a fence. I knew there was no way to avoid hitting the fence as I was thrown off the four-wheeler. It all took place in a moment and the next thing I knew; I could smell fresh cut grass. I love that smell and I was covered in it. I also knew I was severely injured again.

My right arm was completely dead, absolutely no feeling whatsoever. My palm was facing upside down and facing in the wrong direction. I thought I must have broken my arm at the shoulder because of the angle of my arm and hand. I feared my neck was damaged again but was relieved that I could move my toes and legs. I did not move but started yelling for help as loud as I was able. A few minutes later, my brother found me and called 911. We live in a rural location, and I thought it would be a long wait for help to arrive. To my amazement, within five minutes two individuals who lived in my area heard the call on their scanners, got to me before the ambulance, and started working on me. One of the men stabilized my head while the other started cutting off my shirt. The ambulance arrived and I was put on a backboard. Up to that point, I hadn't had any pain as my arm and hand had no feeling. As I was lifted, I screamed with pain. My neck and right shoulder pain became severe. As I rode in the back of the ambulance, every little bump sent a new wave of pain to my neck and shoulder.

Things moved very fast as I was brought to the emergency room. There was a quick exam, many questions, then a CT scan, then an MRI. It was then that I knew something was serious because the nurses were acting differently. I didn't know it at the time, but I lay immobilized in the hospital for a few hours. The hospital had neurosurgeons but none who could do what needed to be done. They found a surgeon who specialized in the procedure that I needed. She introduced herself and then gave me the diagnosis that I didn't want to hear.

"Mr. Judson, you have broken your neck in two places and will need emergency surgery. You are lucky to be alive. We will have to fuse C6 and C7 of your neck."

I thought, *Déjà vu, not again Lord.* I had no choice: before I knew it, I was on my way to surgery.

Hours later, I awoke from surgery. I had to ask the nurse where I was, what had happened to me, and why was I lying there. As she filled me in, reality hit me like a ton of bricks. Another major neck injury, another long rehab ahead of me with no guarantee if I would get the use of my arm back. I was placed in the ICU trauma unit and left alone for the first time since the accident happened. I now had time to replay what had happened over and over in my mind. *Why didn't I just park that machine in the garage? Why did I take that ride?* Another thought crept in my mind: *How can I get through another rehab and recovery?* The last one was so hard; it took everything I had to recover to the level that I had. I was now fifteen years older, and I wasn't starting from a place of health. I was starting from a compromised position from the previous spinal cord injury.

The thought of another long rehab was overwhelming. Not only was the thought of another long rehab from a life-changing accident daunting, but this also happened during the COVID pandemic. I wasn't allowed visitors, not even my wife. I lay there in the dark in ICU and had never felt so alone. Yet as fast as my mind could think about dealing with another devastating setback in my life, another thought flooded my mind. I heard the words, "You have a good life." I pictured my wife, my children, and grandchildren, and an enveloping wave of love overtook my entire being. It was the love of God that surpasses all understanding. I hadn't experienced that feeling of love since my accident fifteen years earlier when I had a direct experience with God's love. If you have ever been in the hospital for a procedure, a nurse will ask you if you would like a warm blanket. That blanket is heated, and you feel this incredible warmth from that blanket. That is how God's love felt to me. I was completely covered in God's warmth and love.

After I had been out of surgery and had experienced another God encounter, my surgeon came in to let me know how the surgery went. I was not prepared for what she told me, because it was so incredible. I wondered why God would allow another accident in my life and I got my answer much quicker than the last time. She started by telling me I was a very lucky man. I could have been dead if the injury was a millimeter in either direction. I could have been completely paralyzed from the neck break, but the story doesn't end there. She said that once she started repairing my neck, she noticed that the original spinal cord injury had never healed. The bone plug never fused after fifteen years, and that I had been walking around with a time bomb in my neck. She then used the "M" word: miracle. It was a miracle because I could have died or been completely paralyzed at any moment. The blessing in this is she was able to repair the shoddy work the "genius" had done many years ago. I couldn't believe what I was hearing. God's hand of protection had covered me all those years, and now I would receive the proper healing I didn't get all that time.

I spent the next six days in the hospital, four of them in the neurotrauma ICU and two on the neurotrauma floor. My neurologist thought that I should stay at a rehab center for a few more days, but I assured her that I could rehab at my local hospital. I wanted to go home and have my wife drive me there. This was, after all, not my first rehab rodeo.

Aside from my right arm being completely paralyzed, I was also having trouble swallowing. My throat was damaged. My vocal cords had been affected, and I couldn't speak for more than a few minutes at a time. This was a big problem for a pastor who must preach a Saturday evening service and two Sunday morning services between two different campuses. I knew there would be many rehab sessions for my arm but hadn't anticipated that I would be doing physical therapy, occupational therapy, and speech therapy.

Once again, the therapists were excellent and helped with my recovery. I had thirty-two therapies for each one of the three areas of recovery—ninety-six sessions of therapy in all.

It was a challenge to get back in my office, but God was good, and I was preaching while wearing a hard neck brace for three months.

This was one of those blessings and cursings that so many go through in life. I was blessed to have been repaired, and cursed, so to speak, with titanium in both knees and three plates and six screws in my neck. All of these, I was told, would develop arthritis.

I was also left with a paralyzed right arm, and I happen to be right-handed. The Lord was giving me an opportunity to work on my left-hand coordination. One of my loves in life is playing guitar and that was out for the time being. The good news was that my neurologist thought that I would gain most of the use in my right arm in about a year to a year and a half.

As I am adding this chapter, it has been seven months since the accident. I have regained about seventy percent use and some feeling in my arm. The shoulder and arm can still be very painful at times as muscles, tendons, ligaments, and nerve endings repair and grow. I have even started playing on the worship teams again as a guitarist and bassist. I just need a little help getting my guitar strapped on.

I was surprised at how much speech therapy was needed and how much it helped. Preaching three services in two days and all the visiting between those services requires about two hundred minutes of speaking. When I first got out of surgery, after twenty minutes my voice became hoarse and I found it painful to speak, but God has healed that also.

Chapter 17

OVERCOMER

*M*any people have faced severe challenges in their lives, some physical, some mental; some suffer loss, some lose everything. My heart goes out to all of them. I can only speak for myself, but I can say without God I would not have made it back. When we hear about someone who has come back from a tragedy, that person is called an overcomer. For me, overcoming came through my faith in God and watching His hand in my life.

The Lord has restored all the material possessions that I had lost. He allows me to function day to day with great independence. He has placed me in a wonderful church where I am the senior pastor. My total time out of the pulpit was seven years the first time and only five weeks the second time. Those times of being out and recovering were the greatest training I have ever received. What did I learn during those times? First would be patience, the ability to wait on God to see what it is He is doing. Prior to the spinal cord injury and then sixteen years later breaking my neck in two places, I would say a brief prayer and take off running trying to make things happen. My greatest joy now is sitting back and watching how God operates. He moves people in and out, situations arise, decisions need to be made, and God is in it all. He always accomplishes what

He needs accomplished, and rarely does He do it how I thought it would happen. I just sit back and am amazed how all things work for good for those who love Him.

Another thing I learned during those years of recovery was to truly trust God. I had always trusted God, but the stakes were never very high. It's easy to trust when there isn't much on the line. This time I had to put all my trust in God. I wasn't physically able to make anything happen on my own; I had to trust God. I placed my trust in Him and He has proven Himself over and over to me.

It's easy to say that you trust God, but it looks very different when it becomes more than lip service. The reality is you can trust Him. You can speak to Him, and He listens.

There have been numerous lessons I have taken away from my injuries—more than I could list. The last lesson I would like to talk about is how God can sustain you.

It has been sixteen years since the spinal cord injury took place, and now I continue to recover from a broken neck. God has sustained me. He sustained me through His infallible word; He sustained me by using His people. When life is altered and there is no quick fix, and you are suddenly put in a long-term situation, you need to be sustained through the difficulties. That is what my relationship with Jesus Christ has done for me. Jesus would do the same for you.

My prayer in writing this book is that some who have had life-altering situations in their lives will find encouragement and hope in these pages. I hope they know that they are loved beyond human understanding. Whether we are physically able or not, we are loved and can love God. He will take us through whatever we are going through.

I also pray that someone who reads this book will stop trying to run from God and will come into a relationship with Jesus Christ. I am not a believer in chance. If you are reading this now, know God loves you and wants a relationship with you. You may be asking yourself how that can be. Maybe you feel you are too far gone, have committed too many sins, or that God would never accept you. I would like you to know that is a lie. God sent His only begotten Son into the world so all who believe in Him would be saved. If you repent of sin, turn away from it, turn toward God, ask for forgiveness, and believe that Jesus was crucified for your sin, died, was placed in a tomb, and rose three days later giving life over death, you can be saved. But you must believe. I encourage you to do that. If you do, you will find a Savior who will walk you through whatever your situation is. He will never abandon you and will guide you to Himself.

I close this book asking God's blessing on every person who reads it. I want to give God all the glory for every step that I take, every breath that I breathe, and everything in my life. I would be nothing, I came from nothing and would have nothing were it not for the incredible love and grace of Jesus Christ.

To God be the Glory!

Printed in the United States
by Baker & Taylor Publisher Services